Bear Creek Diaries

Poems along a country road in North Carolina

Syndi Witte Holmes

Dedicated to the eternal memory of
Penny Church Gassett

   Penny unfailingly maintained her faith, her grace, her wit, her deep love of her family and friends, and her wonderfully wide smile in spite of the physical toll and suffering that diabetes inflicted on her. The legacy she left all of us who knew and love her includes her beloved family, her mother, Joan Church and her sons, Ritchie and Bobby.
   The Church - Gassett family opened their home and their lives to us when my son and I lived in North Carolina; they are a second family to us and will be in our hearts forever.

Waking Up On a Winter Morning

A night-time snow in North Carolina
is like a surprise birthday party;
waking with splendid awe
to an imperfect landscape now transformed
into the ermine of angels.
Crystallised limbs refract the early sun,
and pine boughs whitened with cradles of snow
dip gently down.

Obligations

Sitting at my computer
trying to write some poems,
I watch the birds scrounge
for seeds left over from the squirrels' breakfasting.
Later, a cardinal hopping onto the patio table,
looks intently through the pane,
urgently issuing telepathic messages
until my attention is fully gained;
"the feeders are empty, stop writing, feed us" he demands.
Leaving my chair, I go to fulfill my obligations.

A Morning Dash

With the pups attempting to ferret out
his hiding space,
the cobalt salamander makes a wild dash,
scampering between my feet,
his long slender tail slapping against my skin,
he pushes his yellow striped body into the crack of a red tile
claiming sanctuary.

In Cartier's Garden of Jewels

Yellow gold and orange tiffany window winged butterflies
flit among the long fluted amethyst blossoms;
sapphires of blue birds, rubied cardinals, opal breasted doves
and burnished copper busted cowbirds
pick through the alabaster lined ebony seeds
that lie amid the emerald blades of grass
at the base of the maple standing guard over its treasures.

Camouflage

The small dark green tree frog
clung motionlessly to the white siding of the house,
hoping his breathing would not betray him,
hoping that shadows cast by the evening's waning light
would offer him refuge, leaving his presence unnoticed
to sing another song into the night.

Faire Bird

Like a fairy from the otherworld,
the hummingbird slips out of a fold in time,
appearing instantaneously
to sip red nectar at the feeder
before disappearing into the ether.
Only the noise of the furious buzz of his wings,
resounding in his wake,
bears witness to his presence
as he propels back into another dimension.

First Steps

In the early spring fields
youngest calves taking first tentative steps on untested legs
balance with uncertainty on uneven soil ,
gradually enlarging their circles of exploration,
moving away from anxious mothers.

Cows Asleep Under Cedars

In the center of the field, under the cedars,
the cows sleep
with the soundness borne of security in numbers.
Their large stocky black forms huddle together
in the early morning's chill,
their exhaled breathe forming
small clouds around their slumbering faces.

Chasing Away the Moon

The moon, translucent in the bluish dawn,
is loathe to relinquish her perch,
having held court all the night with the
attendant raccoons, owls, bats and moths.
The sun's strengthening rays, eager to begin their rule,
jealous of sharing the sky,
push her to leave
on the coattails of the receding night.

By Silken Threads

The slender stalk,
grown tall since the last mowing of the hay,
bent indiscernibly under the weight
of the morning's dew;
a barely there spider's web
tethered to its tip
like a sail to the mast.

It is a lesson we should know-
we are as fragilely tethered to life
as the silken strands are to the blade
and as easily blown away in the hard wind.

A Red-Tail Hawk

Deferring to no man
with a surety born from the innate confidence
of absolute perfection
he waltzes above the trees and highways
on unseen lanes of air with his mate.
The earthbound can only envy with awe
such freedom and lightness.

Night Walk

The starless sky,
obscured by clouds heavily weighted, promises rain;
amid the growing cornstalks and
hovering above the unmown hay
the fireflies dance
to the discordant chorus of the frogs.

In nearby woodlots,
deer fashion pine needle pallets for sleep,
feral cats begin their nightly stalkings,
raccoons and owls stir in dark adventure
while bats swoop between the scattered street lamps,
attracted by the swarmings of bugs.

Pheiddeppides' Run

I cannot imagine
what would have prompted that little earthworm
to leave the comfort of the soft, cool dew covered grass,
to venture out
onto the rough asphalt of the warming road that morning
on such an exceedingly perilous journey.
So openly exposed,
to be picked off as a meal
by any one of the numerous birds sitting on the overhead line
and equally vulnerable
to being run over by the tires of an oncoming vehicle,
unknowingly extinguished.

By the time I became aware of him,
he had nearly made his way across both lanes of the road.
I took it upon myself
to safe guard the last portion of his journey;
he had worked so hard and come so far.
He moved as swiftly as an earthworm can,
hunching his body and pushing forward
until he slid, safely, into a clump of clover and disappeared.
I wonder if he felt an adrenaline rush
as he broke the winner's ribbon
that announced his moment of victory.

The Duchesses Morosini

The spiders weave like Venetian lace makers,
ethereal creations loomed on thin blades of grass
interwoven with rhinestones of dew
that catch the glimmers of the rising sun
to gift the newest dawn.

New York Violation 240.20

White smoke rises over the pond
as a pair of Canada geese slip off the bank
into the water for a morning constitutional.
Perhaps startled by the water's chill
or just reviving the previous day's dispute,
they raise their voices contentiously,
argumentative strains echo across
the bumps of hills that break the rolling of the fields.

The crows, roused from sleep,
in the nearby stand of pines,
scream like angry tenement dwellers
for the geese to shut up.
Then, as if to harass the crows,
the bullfrogs add their bass chorus to the rising din.
In an unseen field across the lane,
a wakened donkey brays his annoyance
while a horse neighs for quiet.

Suddenly there is quiet;
the geese finish their swim in silence
and everyone else resettles into bed
for the sun has yet to break the dawn.

The Sparrow

The perfect small form
of the brown sparrow
lay still and undisturbed
on the white pebbles
of the garden path.

He had made
the world a place of beauty
with his song and his presence.
He had led a purposed life
and died peaceful with his time.

In the quiet,
with the flowers and butterflies
as witnesses to his going,
the wind gathered his breathe
and swept it upward into the clouds.

I slipped him into his final nest,
lamenting his passage with a
commendation of his spirit to Heaven,
to grace another time and space.

Brevity

The exquisiteness of her colour and design
wait to be revealed as the incubating warmth of the sun
cajoles her reluctant blossoming.
She will revel in her moment of beauty,
knowing how quickly her brilliance will fade
in the harshness of the midday glare,
and with the setting of the sun
she will be gone.

Samhein Evening

Into the quiet
the sun resigns its light to the coming night
sliding over the ridges onto a different shore.
The birds retire to limb and brush,
leaving the owls to the third-shift watch.
Frogs, debuting from behind the opening drawing of the clouds,
serenade the rising moon
while whispering wisps of wind
gently rustle the leaves in light applause.

The deepening dark bestows a transcending calm
as the ancients walk through the veil,
speaking words long lost to the ear
but known to the heart.
Words reverberate throughout the soul;
quickening echoes within every membrane of every cell
bind us to the past, to the future, and to eternity.

Rendezvous of Seasons

Summer rushes headlong down the corridor of seasons,
flinging days aside with careless abandon,
ignoring all pleas to slow her pace.
Autumn waits in the wings for her brief time of coloured glory
while winter breathes its frosted breathe,
eager to rush the starting gate,
hold the earth in cryogenic suspension,
and make less space for spring.

The Suddenness of Her Departure

The doe lay in the newly harvested hayfield,
big brown eyes open,
still holding the look of her characteristic inquisitiveness within
yet startled by the suddenness of her demise
by some relentless driver who needed to be somewhere fast.
Her peaceful gaze belied the fact
that a flock of vultures were now tearing at her soft underbelly
with the urgent determination of steely undertakers
completing the work of death.

Reprieve

The black box,
frozen in the middle of the road by the approach of the car,
realised too late that this had not been a good idea.
Seeing it, the car swerved and braked a little beyond the box.
The turtle, startled as the driver picked him up,
attempted to withdraw his head into the deepest recesses of his shell
expecting his demise.
Instead, he found himself set down amid the tall grass
on the side of the road where he had been headed.
He did not move for awhile, unsure of the reprieve,
then accepting the day's grace, moved on.

Labour Day

The hummingbird feeder hangs unused
in the morning shade of the maple;
butterfly bushes stand abandoned in the garden, and
crows sit high in the thinning boughs,
surveying harvested fields for gleanings
as the school bus returns to its route
waving good bye to summer.

Eulogy to a Little Gray Squirrel

I came home today
to find you dead along the roadside,
another victim of a thoughtless driver.

You gave me countless hours of pleasure,
watching as you and your siblings
ate peaceably at the feeder alongside sparrows and cardinals,
ran spirals around the tree's trunk in playful games of chase,
and scurried into the highest branches
when the pups came running outside
for their morning constitutionals,
teasing the bemused, earthbound pups with your
effortless acrobatic jumps from tree to tree.

I could not leave you there as nameless road kill,
to be further defiled;
preparing a bed in the soft earth under the limbs
where you lived and played,
 I laid you in your bed and gave you to God's keeping.
This evening, though the feeders are full,
no bird or sibling has come to eat;
they know you are not there and mourn.
The setting sun kisses your rest
and moonbeams come to guard your sleep

Mid-November Morning Walk in the North Carolina Countryside

The fierce winds of several nights ago
have forcibly evicted most of the leaves still clinging to their perches.
Stark, dark limbs standing out against the graying skies
bring November into sharp focus ;
all traces of summer and autumn are now eradicated
as winter taps incessantly at the door.

The sun rises late.
In the distance, retorts from a shotgun
break the early morning silence,
announcing the presence of a hopeful hunter.
Wood burnings incense the air,
smoke curls lull on the chimney's ledge
in the coolness of the dawn.

In nearby woods, safe from the hunter's stalking,
unseen creatures begin to stir in the underbrush,
their steps crackling on dried leaves.
Birds assume their posts on telephone wires and fences watching
as a flock of geese loudly cross the sky,
moving from one harvested field to another
in search of breakfast amid the fallen stalks.

Winter in the Woods

Descending slowly, softly as down,
the snow seeps among the crevices,
delineating every usually hidden feature
on the floor of the wooded hillside.
The forgotten contours of every fallen leaf,
every dried blade of grass are
once again brought into view.
Outstretched limbs outlined in white,
catch the falling flakes.
Tracks swiftly erased
as the crystalline droplets fall, picking up speed as they go,
eradicate our most recent presence.
Every creature seeks the warmth
of burrows and dens.
All is silent as the snow falls into the night.